TAMBOUR BEADING
with a ring frame

TAMBOUR BEADING
with a ring frame

Maisie Jarratt

Kangaroo Press

Acknowledgments

My thanks to those who have helped me in compiling this book—for photography, Tim Wade of Nowra; for typing, Debra Moore of Gerringong; and for overall support, my husband Duncan Jarratt.

First published in 1994 by Kangaroo Press Pty Ltd
3 Whitehall Road Kenthurst NSW 2156 Australia
P.O. Box 6125 Dural Delivery Centre NSW 2158
Typeset by G.T. Setters Pty Limited
Printed in Hong Kong through Colorcraft Ltd

ISBN 0 86417 646 5

CONTENTS

INTRODUCTION

This book follows on from my three previous books, *French Embroidery Beading: How to Bead, Embroidery Beading: Designs and Techniques* and *Embroidery Beading with Australian Native Flowers, Birds and Butterflies*, all published by Kangaroo Press. This book is a complete work on tambour beading and explains the basic techniques and methods used.

The book was originally planed to cover only tambour beading in a ring frame, with small designs and motifs, but enthusiasm got the better of me and I have included three projects for the larger rectangular tambour frame, along with complete instructions for making the frame. Several of the ring frame projects can also be worked on the rectangular frame if you prefer.

Designs include beaded tops and expensive-looking Victorian evening bags as well as numerous smaller designs and motifs that can be beaded separately and appliquéd to previously completed garments.

I have spent many years of my life beading garments by hand by the tambour method. Truly exciting designs can be created on the tambour, from a simple motif to a fully beaded gown.

At the age of fifteen I first learnt this lovely art from a wonderful French woman. Mastering the technique very quickly, I was soon beading full length gowns all over in her workroom.

After World War I the Flapper era was ushered in with lots of fringing and bugle beads; grandmothers found themselves sitting and beading for hours. I started working between the two world wars and have seen a lot of changes in beadwork over the years. During World War II there were very few beads available and as a result I could only use secondhand beads sold in department stores. I would wash them in Persil and end up with enough sparkling beads to make pretty beaded collars on satin. After the war imports started to flow into the country from Europe. Beautifully cut beads, pearls and crystals were then available.

Beading in the 1920s and 1930s was worked very flat on the fabric, on beautiful pure silks and laces. Then a new technique was born. All the manufacturers and order-workrooms wanted a three-dimensional look, chunky beads sewn together one on top of the other, and beading became very heavy. With the tambour technique the beads also had to be embroidered in a raised fashion—I would sit many days, and nights until the early hours of the morning, beading to finish a gown that would be worn to a special function or ball.

Even after fifty-five years of beading, I still love to idle away hours at my frame working out samples and designs. Now, as the years pass, I am enjoying writing about all I have embroidered, passing my knowledge on to others.

I have taught many women this lovely art in the workrooms. Being blessed with good hands and wonderful eyesight I hope to continue for many years yet.

Maisie Jarratt, 1994

HISTORY OF TAMBOUR BEADING

In the early 1920s French embroiderers discovered that the Cornaly needle, fitted into a special holder, could be used for bead embroidery. Working by hand, using a chain stitch to hold beads and sequins in place on fabric stretched over a tambour frame was found to be a very fast method of working with beads.

The Cornaly needle is very much like a fine crochet hook, the difference being a tiny curve on the open side of the hook. This keeps the thread in place while working the chain stitch.

Tambouring takes its name from the circular frame resembling the top of a *tambour* (French for a large drum), used also for thread embroidery. A rectangular tambour frame was also designed to hold larger pieces of fabric taut. Using these frames the beading can be worked using both hands. The thread works the chain stitch from the top (the wrong side of the fabric is uppermost), the other hand taking the beads underneath the frame to the right side of the fabric.

The Cornaly needle used for tambour beading takes its name from its origins as the needle used in the French Cornaly embroidery machine. This machine was used for all kinds of chain stitch embroidery from the early 1920s to the late 1950s, a period when flowers and scrolls were popular decorations on linen and crepe gowns. The Cornaly machine is no longer in use, superseded by a new generation of embroidery machines.

EQUIPMENT AND TECHNIQUES

Ring frame

Ring frames (embroidery and quilting frames) vary in size from 30 cm to 50 cm (12'' to 20''), and are most suitable for beading motifs or small designs. These frames can be readily purchased from craft shops.

Rectangular frame

Rectangular frames are used for garments with heavier all-over designs. They are simple free-standing frames which will have to be made to specific measurements by a handyperson, as they are unavailable commercially. Instructions and measurements are given on pages 47–48.

The Cornaly needle and holder

The Cornaly needle is a long needle originally used in the Cornaly embroidery machine. To adapt it for bead embroidery it is cut and fitted into a holder 25 mm long made from a length of solid brass rod 5 mm thick. The last 5 mm is machined to a taper. A very fine drill is used to make a central hole to fit the cut Cornaly needle, with another hole at right angles on the side of the brass, made with a fine thread for a tiny jeweller's screw to hold the needle in place. A fine wooden pen-like handle is then fitted to the brass holder. A jeweller or an instrument maker can easily make such a holder, following these instructions and guided by the photograph. Insert the needle into the holder with the open part of the needle facing the screw—this is your guide when working the chain stitch on the tambour frame.

Cornaly needles (with handles) are imported from Europe and are available in 4 sizes—very fine, fine, medium and thick—from Australian suppliers (see page 72).

1. *Very fine* is used for bead and sequin work on fabrics such as chiffons and organzas.
2. *Fine* and *medium* are used for linen type fabrics.
3. *Thick* is used for applying fine wool, cotton, metallic thread, etc., to heavier fabrics.

Once you have learnt this fine craft, the great advantage of using the tambour technique for embroidery beading and sequin work is that you can cover a large area with beads and sequins in a short time. I am able to embroider a whole blouse, of the sort shown in this book, including fringing, in six working days. A short tunic frock beaded all over, with fringing around the hemline, would take 10 to 14 working days to bead.

Another advantage of tambour beading is that beads can be spaced evenly with no trouble and sequins can be attached closely together.

Learning to tambour bead takes time and patience, but once you have mastered the technique you will not want to leave the beads alone! Time will disappear as you work out samples and create wonderful beadwork designs.

Setting up the ring frame

Use a ring frame (embroidery or quilt) for your tambour beading if you are embroidering collars, Victorian evening bags, motifs or any garment trim. They are available in sizes from 20 cm to 50 cm

A pair of the Cornaly needles used for tambour beading resting on a selection of beads

A large ring frame (page 8) and a rectangular frame (page 47) set up for tambour beading

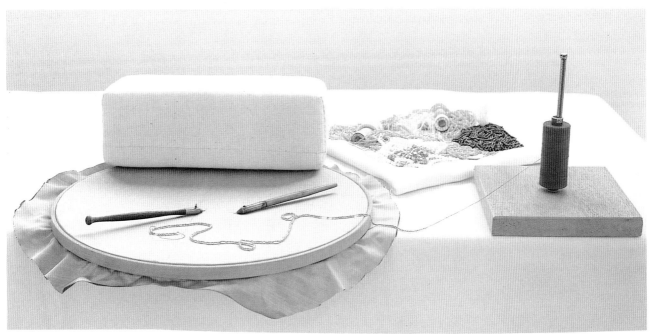

*Ring frame set up on table edge with brick
weight in position (page 15)*

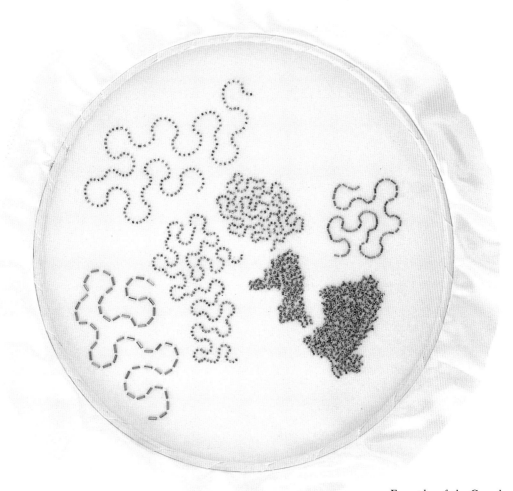

*Examples of the Cornaly crazy design
worked with different beads (page 16)*

The finished sample motif (page 18). The top picture shows the work from the wrong side (or top) as it appears while you are beading; the second picture shows the right side (or bottom)

(12''–20'') from craft shops for a very modest price (approximately $3.50 to $7.95).

The ring frame can be handled very easily, is portable and is easily repositioned as you work. To keep it steady on the work surface I use a fabric-covered house brick (see photograph).

You will also need a spool-holder, easily made by hammering a 13 cm (5'') round-head nail into the centre of a 15 cm (6'') square block of wood 2.5 cm (1'') thick.

13 cm (5") nail

15 cm (6") square
2.5 cm (1") thick

1. Before you start, cut a long strip of calico on the bias, 3 cm (1¼'') wide. Unscrew the ring frame and bind the calico around the inner ring of the frame, keeping the calico smooth. This will grip the fabric to the frame while you work.
2. I always tell beginners to start off their practice pieces on a piece of organza fabric. This way you will be able to see your work through the fabric when making the chain stitch.
3. Tambour beading is worked from the wrong side of the fabric. That is, the beads are underneath, the right side of the fabric is underneath and the wrong side of the fabric is always on top, facing you.
4. Lay the fabric over the inner ring with the calico binding, centring the grain. Fit the outer ring over the fabric, easing the fabric all round until it is taut. Ensure that both grains are even, then tighten the screw. Always keep the fabric very taut.
5. Keep the ring frame in position on the edge of the table with the covered brick, resting it on the table and on the edge of the ring frame. This supports the frame, leaving both hands free to work.
6. Place a spool of free-running thread on the spool-holder and the beads on the left side of your work (on the right if you are left-handed). As most beads come on string, tie the bead-string to the free-running thread with a slip-knot and slide the beads over the knot. Discard the bead-string.

When threading sequins, thread with the right side, i.e. cup side, hanging downwards.

See photograph on page 11.

Working the chain stitch

1. Set up the ring frame using a piece of fine transparent organza.
2. Use thread only to begin with until you have mastered the chain stitch and become familiar with the tambour needle.
3. Be prepared to do a lot of practice to perfect the technique of turning the needle in all directions.
4. Work on the wrong side of the fabric with a spool of free-running thread on the left-hand side. (A left-handed person will have the thread on the right side.)
5. Hold the thread between the left thumb and forefinger underneath the frame. With the tambour holder and needle in the right hand, insert the needle vertically through the fabric, with the screw facing away to the right. Always use the screw as a guide to the needle's position.
6. Slide the tambour needle between the thumb and forefinger, picking up the thread. Holding the thread, turn and raise the hook anticlockwise, keeping the holder in the upright position, then draw the loop through the fabric to make the chain stitch.
7. The turn of the needle prevents it snagging the fabric as you bring the needle up.
8. Insert the needle inside the loop and pull up the next stitch in the chain to the right, working a short distance from the first stitch. The length of the chain stitch is varied according to the sizes of the beads or sequins that are being used.

As you progress with the needle you should be able to work in all directions without turning the frame. This will take a lot of practice, always watching the turn of the needle as you bring the loop through the fabric to make the chain stitch. Once you have mastered working in all directions you should be able to work at high speed.
9. Work with the right tension, moving the thread up to the fabric. If you pull the thread too tight you will not be able to form a loop easily. If you work too loosely the thread will be floppy and the stitches will hang away from the fabric.
10. Once you feel happy with the chain stitch, move on to practising with beads or sequins. Always start with 2 tiny chain stitches (thread only) and pull tight. When completing each beaded section, make 2 tiny chain stitches (thread only). Break the thread underneath the frame, pull through the chain stitch and pull firm. This will anchor the beading.
11. Do not thread more than about 1 metre (40'') of beads at any one time. This way, if there happened

to be an accident with the thread on the gown, only a small amount of the chain would run.

12. Sequins are threaded right side up (or cup side up) hanging down on the thread. When the chain stitch is worked the sequin is facing the right side up. Use a chain stitch half the size of the sequin. That way the sequins will overlap each other.

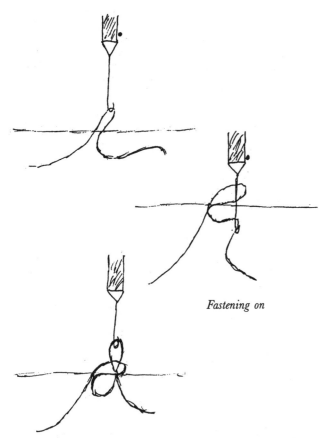

Fastening on

13. When you are beading with size 2 and size 3 bugle beads, always use a support stitch after each bead (thread only). This way the bead will lie firm on the fabric. The same applies to beading with 3 or 4 beads at a time in zigzag fashion—use a support stitch. If you are working with the beads raised-up the support stitch is needed for that as well.

14. To give added lustre to sequin work use silver or gold metallic thread. You would then use a medium-size tambour needle.

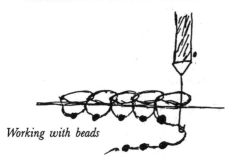

Working with beads

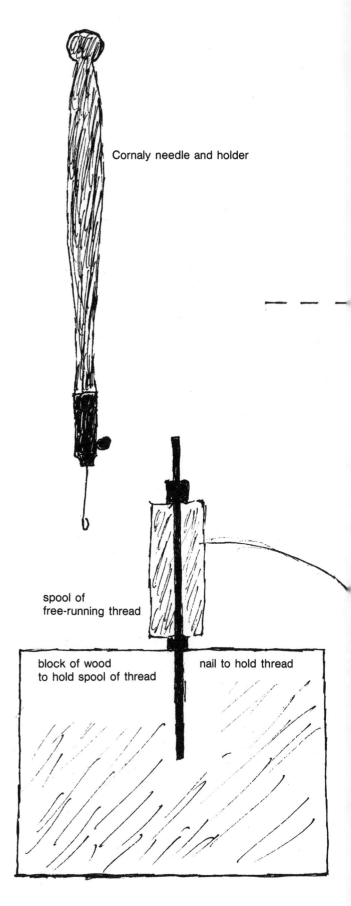

Cornaly needle and holder

spool of
free-running thread

block of wood
to hold spool of thread

nail to hold thread

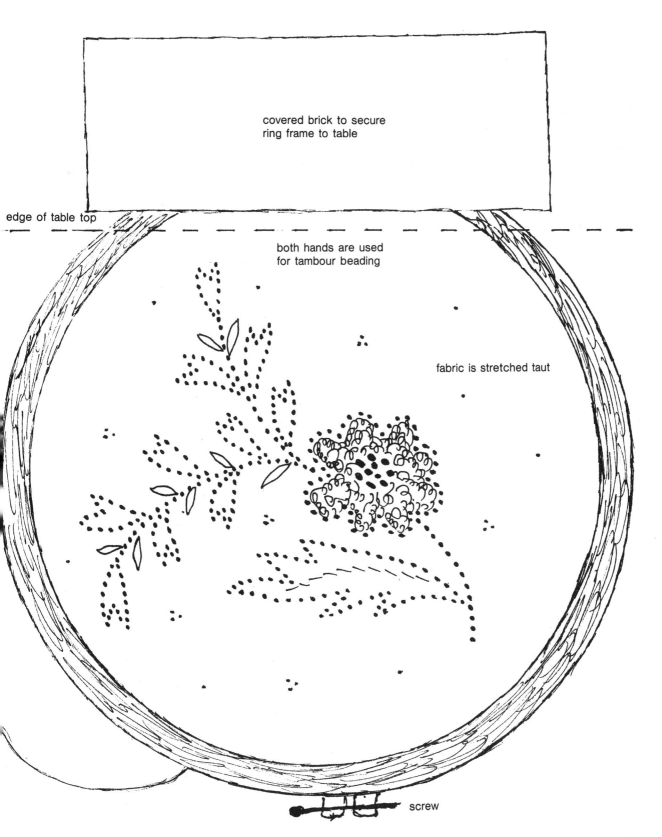

covered brick to secure
ring frame to table

edge of table top

both hands are used
for tambour beading

fabric is stretched taut

screw

The tambour Cornaly crazy design

1. Once you have learned to turn the needle in all directions you will be able to work the Cornaly 'crazy' design. It is very important to learn this freehand design as it comes into all tambour beading. Work in steps from the large patterns down to the medium and close-work designs.

   Close-work is used in many designs to cover small and large areas of beading. It must be learned at the beginning.

   The photograph shows the various sizes of 'crazy' designs and the different sized beads used in them. If you are working with size 3 bugle beads or larger note that you must make a support stitch after *each* bead is worked.

Large design
2. Just imagine you are working around in a half-circle and breaking off into another half-circle. With practice this will become very easy. It is a good idea to sketch in a few swirls until you have mastered the feel of working freehand.

Medium design
3. This follows the same procedure as the large crazy design but reduces the size of the half-circles. This is also used for filling-in large areas of beading.

Small design
4. When working with the small covering design, try working as if you were making triangles or small squares. Work 1 bead on each single tambour stitch to form a square.

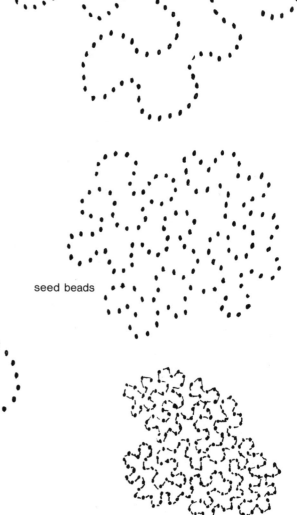

seed beads

close work

Crazy designs

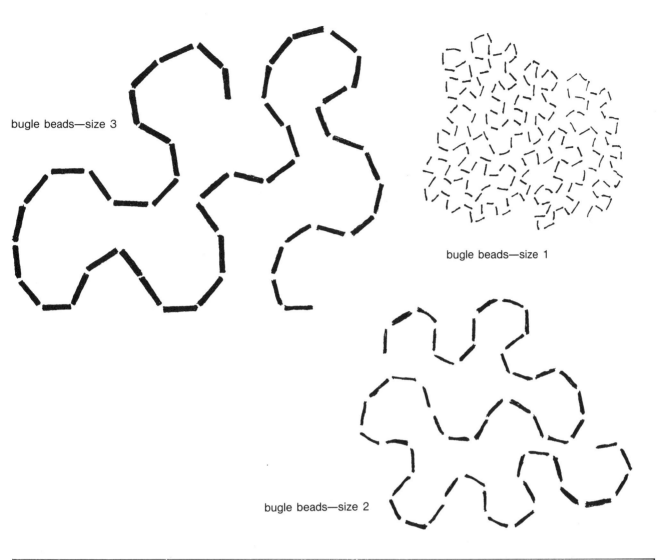

bugle beads—size 3

bugle beads—size 1

bugle beads—size 2

HANDY HINTS

Tracing a design

1. Sketch out the design you wish to embroider on tracing paper with firm, bold lines, and transfer it to the fabric using a fade-out pencil.
2. It is a good idea to run a tacking thread around the design. If the pencil fades away while you are working the design the thread saves a lot of retracing. The thread can be pulled out when the beading is completed.
3. Collect the different beads and sequins needed for the design before you start.
4. If you are uncertain of your bead choices, sew a few beads and sequins onto a small sample of the fabric to see how they suit the design and the material.

Washing instructions

1. Hand wash beaded garments in cold water with Softly or a wool wash.
2. Rinse and drip dry in the shade.
3. Iron on the wrong side of the garment with the beading resting on a towel—press on a warm iron setting only.
4. DO NOT wash in a machine or tumble dry.

Checking colourfastness

Be sure the beads you choose are colourfast. On some glass beads the colour washes off, leaving you with just a clear glass bead. Always test by mixing a teaspoon of Softly in a cupful of water and leaving the beads to soak for about 20 minutes. Rinse. If the beads stand this test they are colourfast.

TAMBOUR BEADING A SMALL MOTIF

1. Tambour beading a small design to trim a garment can be done quite easily. Small collars and trimmings added to a plain dress or blouse can smarten it up dramatically. A motif can be beaded onto silk, lace or any suitable fabric and embroidered on either a ring frame or a rectangular frame, and later appliqued to the garment.

2. Select a fabric and trace the rosebud from page 19 onto the wrong side. Cut the fabric to the required size and lay it right side up on a larger, square piece of calico. Match the fabric grains vertically and horizontally—this way when stretched onto the tambour frame they will stretch evenly. Pin and stitch together by machine.

3. Cut the centre of the calico away, leaving 2 cm (¾'') inside the lines of machine stitching. Be careful not to cut into the piece of fabric to be beaded. Snip into each corner of the calico so the sides can be turned back when beading. See sketch. Fix the fabric into the ring frame following the instructions on page 8. (If you are using a rectangular frame, see page 47 for detailed instructions on setting up the fabric.)

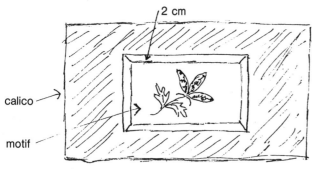

4. It is possible to embroider garments already made up, although it is not as easy and not all garments are suitable. This can only be done on a ring frame.

5. If you are using a stretch knit fabric, do not stretch it too tightly on the frame as it is likely to bounce back and pucker when released. A very fine interfacing can be used to solve the problem. A good quality double-knit jersey is safe to tambour bead onto as it does not have as much stretch as single-knit jersey. This is what I used when beading the sample motif (see the photographs on page 12).

Rosebud sample motif

The rosebud motif, a simple motif a beginner could bead, can be worked on a ring frame or rectangular frame. One or two of these buds would sparkle on a sweater or blouse.

You will need
Pink seed beads
A few cerise seed beads
Pale green seed beads
Matching thread
Dressmaker's carbon paper

Method
1. Once the fabric is set up, thread the green beads onto the free-running thread on the left of the ring frame, using the holder described on page 13, or one of the nails on the left of the rectangular frame (page 46).

2. Trace the rosebud motif onto the wrong side of the fabric facing you.

3. Bead the stem of the rosebud with single beads, starting from the bud and working down. Holding

the thread in the left hand between the thumb and forefinger underneath the frame, and the tambour holder and needle in the right hand, insert the needle through the fabric, holding it upright, and pull the thread up to the wrong side. Hold and make 2 tiny chain stitches to anchor using thread only.

4. Moving the beads underneath up to the fabric, insert the needle again and make a chain stitch the size of the green bead. Pick up the thread between each bead, turning the needle as you do so. Continue with each bead, pointing the needle along the stem using the screw as your guide.

5. Finish the stem by making 2 tiny chain stitches, thread only. Break the thread underneath, pull the thread through the chain stitch and pull tight to anchor.

6. Bead each leaf with single beads, starting each leaf from the stem. Bead the vein inside the leaf.

7. Thread the pink beads for the bud on the free-running thread. Insert the needle at the base of the rosebud. Bead single beads all around the outside petals. Thread the cerise beads and bead the centre line of the bud. Outline this with single beads, then fill in with the close Cornaly design.

8. Return with the pink beads, beading the top section of the rose petal. Outline with pink beads then fill in with the close Cornaly design.

9. Bead the tiny leaves coming from the base of the bud with 2 rows of green seed beads.

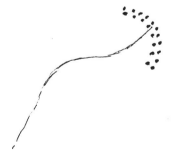

10. The finished sample appears on page 12, the two photographs showing the back (top surface) of the work, and the front (bottom surface).

RING FRAME PROJECTS

1. Rose motif

Illustrated on page 37

A delightful pink rose motif to adorn a blouse or sweater.

You will need

36 cm (14'') ring frame
Green seed beads
Pale pink 3-cut seed beads
Dark pink 3-cut seed beads
Cerise 3-cut seed beads
Fabric of choice
Carbon tracing paper
Matching thread

Method

1. Assemble the ring frame with the front panel of a blouse or sweater. *Do not cut out.* Lay the fabric on the inner section of the ring, centring the grain with the wrong side of the fabric facing you. Place the outer section onto the fabric and stretch taut, ensuring both grains are evenly stretched.
2. Pin the carbon paper and the rose design in position on the fabric. Lay the ring frame over a raised flat surface and press firmly with a pencil to transfer the design onto the blouse. Secure the ring frame on the edge of the table with the covered brick to balance it.
3. Thread green seed beads onto the free-running thread from the holder on your left side. Work these beads singly on the stems, leaves and buds.

    Firstly bead the rose stem. With the thread underneath in your left hand, and starting from the top of the stem, insert the tambour needle, pull the thread through to the wrong side then hold.
4. Make 2 tiny chain stitches (thread only) to anchor.

Make another chain stitch the size of the bead. Continue placing each bead for the stem. Anchor with 2 tiny chain stitches, break the thread underneath and pull it firmly through the chain. Continue this way around the leaves and the lower section of the buds. See sketch.

5. Thread the dark pink seed beads for the small buds. Work with single beads around the buds and fill in the centres.
6. The large bud has 3 shades of pink worked with single beads. See sketch.
7. The rose bloom has 3 shades of pink worked in each petal. All beads are worked singly.

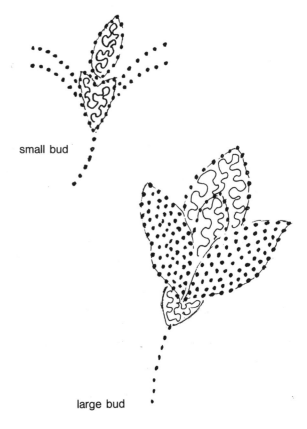

small bud

large bud

20

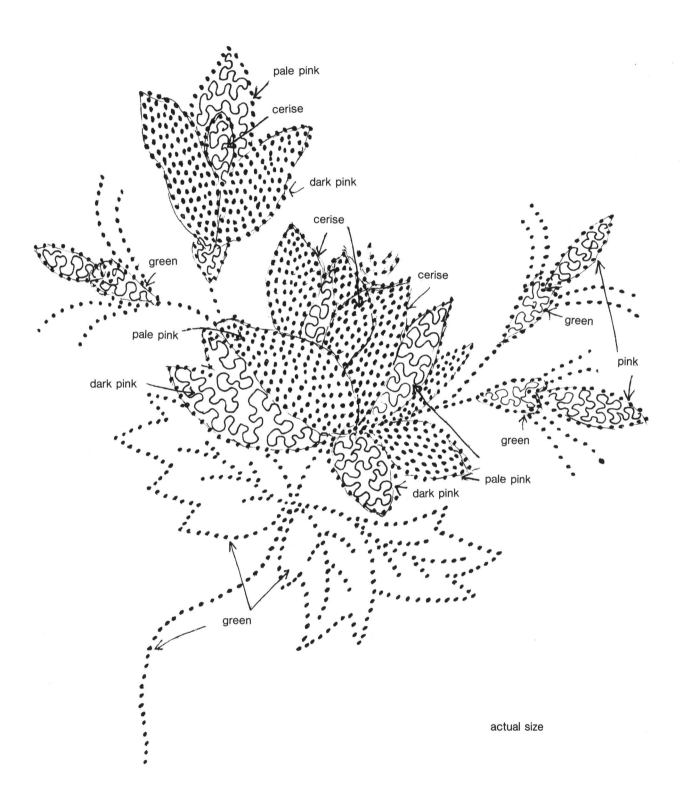

pale pink

cerise

dark pink

cerise

cerise

green

green

pink

pale pink

dark pink

green

pale pink

dark pink

green

actual size

21

2. Spider flower motif

Illustrated on page 21

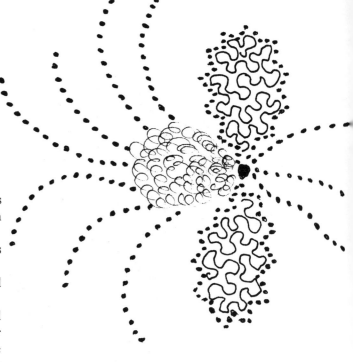

You will need

36 cm (14'') ring frame
Blue 3-cut seed beads
Blue size 2 bugle beads
Blue crystal iridescent cup sequins
Pale blue georgette
Matching thread
Dressmaker's carbon paper

Method

1. Assemble the ring frame following the instructions on page 8, and stretch the blue georgette taut in the frame.
2. Trace the design onto the fabric using dressmaker's carbon paper.
3. Thread the seed beads onto the free-running thread on the spool holder.

    Bead all the stems first in the blue 3-cut seed beads, holding the thread in the left hand under the frame. Insert the tambour needle, pick up the thread and pull through and hold, making 2 tiny chain stitches (thread only) to anchor.
4. Bead 3 beads together all along each stem. Move the 3 beads to the fabric lying flat. Make 1 chain stitch the length of the 3 beads and continue along all the stems. This is a quicker method of applying beads and is very effective.
5. Bead single beads around each leaf, making a chain stitch the size of each seed bead. *Keep the tension even when tambour beading.*
6. Thread the size 2 bugle beads on the working thread. Insert the needle inside the top of the leaf. Pick up the thread and work 2 stitches (thread only). Make a chain stitch the length of the bugle bead and 1 tiny support stitch (thread only).

    Move the needle to the right making a small stitch (2 mm), then another support stitch (thread only). Move another bugle bead, making the stitch the same length as the bead. Continue until you have 6 bugle beads angling downwards through the centre of the leaf, giving a contrast to the leaf.
7. Bead each petal on the outside edge, moving 3 beads at a time, making a zigzag with a small stitch and then a support stitch after each 3 beads to give a picot-edged look in a slightly raised style. Continue around the six petals.

8. The six petals are then filled in with the small Cornaly crazy pattern.
9. Thread 3 pearls and bead one for each centre flower.
10. Work the centre petal with the crystal sequins. Thread these with the cup side facing downwards on the working thread so when sequinned the cup side will be on the right side. Sequin these in rows starting from the outside and working in rows until the petal is completed.

    Make a stitch half the size of the sequin, so that the sequins will overlap.

    Finish each single swirl marked on the design with single beads.

CCCCCC

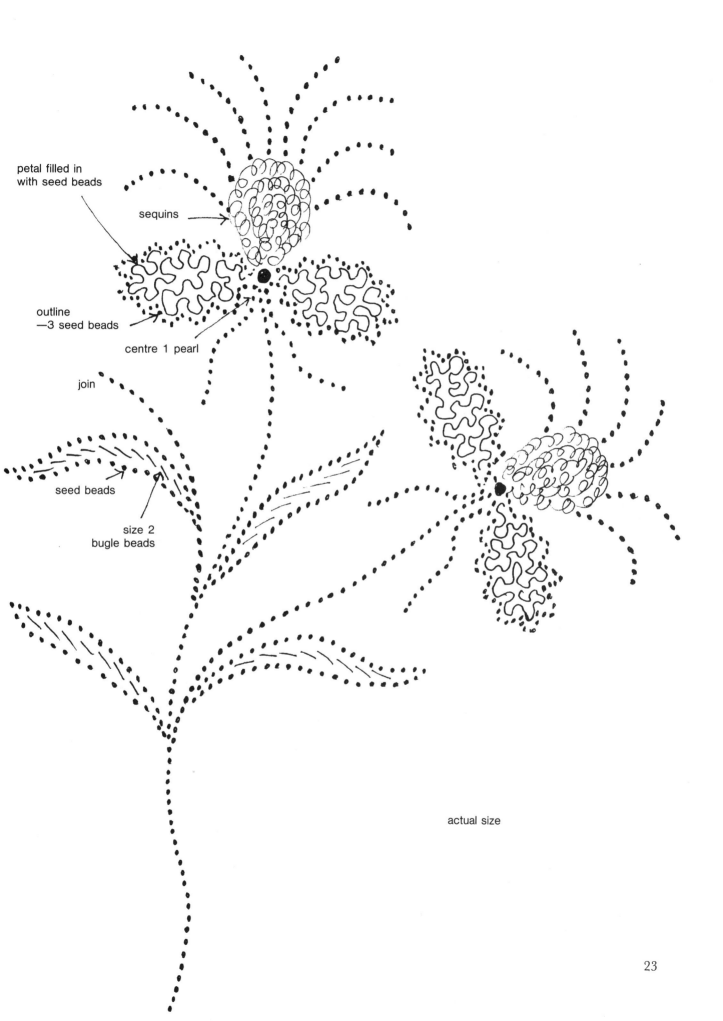

petal filled in
with seed beads

sequins

outline
—3 seed beads

centre 1 pearl

join

seed beads

size 2
bugle beads

actual size

23

3. Wild rose design
Illustrated on page 39

You will need
50 cm (20'') ring frame
0.5 m (½ yd) pale pink Thai silk
Pale pink 3-cut seed beads
Pale pink iridescent cup sequins
Pale pink seed pearls
Pale pink wheat-shaped pearls
Size 2 iridescent bugle beads
Matching thread
Dressmaker's carbon paper

This is one of my designs from early 1960. I have reproduced it here on pale pink pure Thai silk.

This is very simple tambour beading, being all single lines of 1 bead worked singly. The roses are outlined with single beads, then filled in with tiny sequins. Seed pearls are added to the centres of the roses. Small wheat-shaped pearls decorate the stems between each small leaf, angling outwards. Cluster spotting of three beads is added to highlight the design.

I have used pale pink fabric but the colour is really a matter of choice. Beads and sequins should be coordinated with the particular fabric being used.

Note This pattern has had to be reduced to fit in the book, so you will need to enlarge it again by 150% using a photocopying machine or by the grid method at 2 cm = 3 cm (1'' = 1½'').

Note This design can also be worked on the rectangular frame, as shown in the photograph on page 39.

Method
1. Tambour bead this design onto the piece of silk, or embroider it directly onto an evening gown if you prefer. *Do not cut out*, but leave the fabric in one piece and attach it to the ring frame. (Instructions for attaching fabric to the rectangular frame are given on page 47.)
2. Lay the frame over a firm raised surface (a board or a book) to make it easier to transfer the design without stretching the fabric with the pencil. Lay a sheet of carbon paper on the fabric and on top of this place the traced design. Pin and press firmly with a pencil all along the design.
3. Thread the pink seed beads onto the matching free-running thread on the holder on your left. String approximately 1 metre (40'') of beads at a time. Hold your left hand underneath the frame with the

N.B. This pattern must be enlarged

thread between the thumb and forefinger, with the tambour holder and needle in the right hand. Pull the thread through to the wrong side and make 2 tiny chain stitches to anchor (thread only).

Moving 1 seed bead up against the fabric, make 1 chain stitch to the size of the seed bead. Bead all the stem lines on the design with 1 bead worked singly, breaking off the thread and finishing off as you complete each element.

4. Outline all the tiny leaves, rose leaves and flowers with seed beads. Bead veins inside the larger rose leaves, using seed beads and bugle beads. See diagram. All the tips of the larger and smaller leaves have sharp points. As you reach the tip of each point, make a tiny support stitch (thread only). This will keep the point sharply angled.

5. Work 1 row of single seed beads around the edge of each rose flower.

6. Thread the sequins onto the free-running thread with the cup side facing downwards. Work each chain stitch half the size of each sequin as the sequins should overlap. (Remember to make the anchoring stitches before starting and again when finishing each section of beading.) Work the first row of sequins inside the row of beads, then work each row, filling in the rose, leaving a small circle in the centre for the seed pearls.

7. Thread the seed pearls and work these into the centres of the roses.

8. Thread the wheat-shaped pearls onto the working thread. Work each long pearl singly along the stems.

9. Thread more pink seed beads and bead the cluster spotting of 3 beads around the design.

4. Bow motif

Illustrated on page 40

A bow motif is very effective on the front of a blouse or sweater. The centre flower and dangling arrangement are hand beaded when all the tambour beading is completed.

You will need

30 cm (12'') or 36 cm (14'') ring frame
Chunky crystal beads for the basic outline (colour of choice)
Red 3-cut seed beads
6 red 7 mm cut beads
10 red 5 mm cut beads for the centre flower and dangling arrangements
Small amount of red cup sequins for centre flower
Dressmaker's carbon paper
Matching thread

Method

1. Mark out the shape of the garment pattern piece you wish to embroider with a tacking thread. *Do not cut out.* With the fabric wrong side up, position the traced bow design and mark the centre point with a pin. Assemble the fabric into the ring frame, centring the grain. Stretch evenly taut and tighten the screw.
2. Position the carbon paper and traced design on the wrong side of the fabric and press firmly with a pencil to transfer the design.
3. Thread the chunky crystal beads onto the working thread on your left side. These beads do not always come threaded on strings so you will have to thread the amount you require by hand onto the working thread.
4. Secure the ring frame to the edge of the table with the covered brick to hold it firm. With the thread in your left hand underneath the ring frame and the tambour needle in the right hand, insert the needle into the top section of the bow. Make 2 tiny chain stitches (thread only) to anchor. Make a further chain stitch the size of a chunky bead and attach bead. Continue around the 3 parts of the bow, leaving a 2 cm (¾'') square space in the centre for the sequin flower to be worked.
5. Work all around the leaves with single crystal beads in the same manner.
6. Use red seed beads, worked singly, on the scrolls and on the lines angling downwards between the 2 leaves on each side. Work red beads singly inside

the leaves with 4 beads angling outwards on the small veins. See sketch.

7. With the red seed beads, return to the top section of the bow and insert the needle with 2 stitches to anchor. Move 4 beads together working in a zigzag fashion over the row of crystal beads. Work a tiny

support stitch (thread only) after each 4 beads to hold firm. This will give a three-dimensional look.
8. Continue the zigzag until all the bow and leaf outlines are worked over, leaving the scrolls with the single red beads for a contrast.
9. Using the red seed beads work the crazy design in the open spaces of the bow.

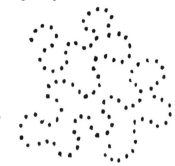

10. Return to the scrolls and bead the short lines angling outwards with 4 red seed beads.
11. To start the centre flower, sew a red 7 mm cut bead in the centre, sewing twice through with double thread. Loop 7 red seed beads four times around this bead. Thread together 3 red seed beads, 1 sequin (cup side up), 1 seed bead, 1 sequin, 1 seed bead and 1 sequin and work these outwards from the centre bead 4 times.

    Insert the bead needle back to the centre bead. Thread together 3 seed beads, 1 sequin, 1 seed bead and 1 sequin and sew these twice between each of the 4 longer sections you have just finished beading. Make a support stitch after each row of sequins. Do not take the beads and sequins too far out from the centre bead as they will become loose. Keep firm.

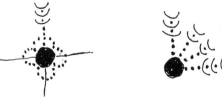

12. Finish by sewing on the dangling arrangements, following the sketch. Use 4 strands of thread with these hanging beads as glass beads can cut the thread with wear.

Bow motif

actual size

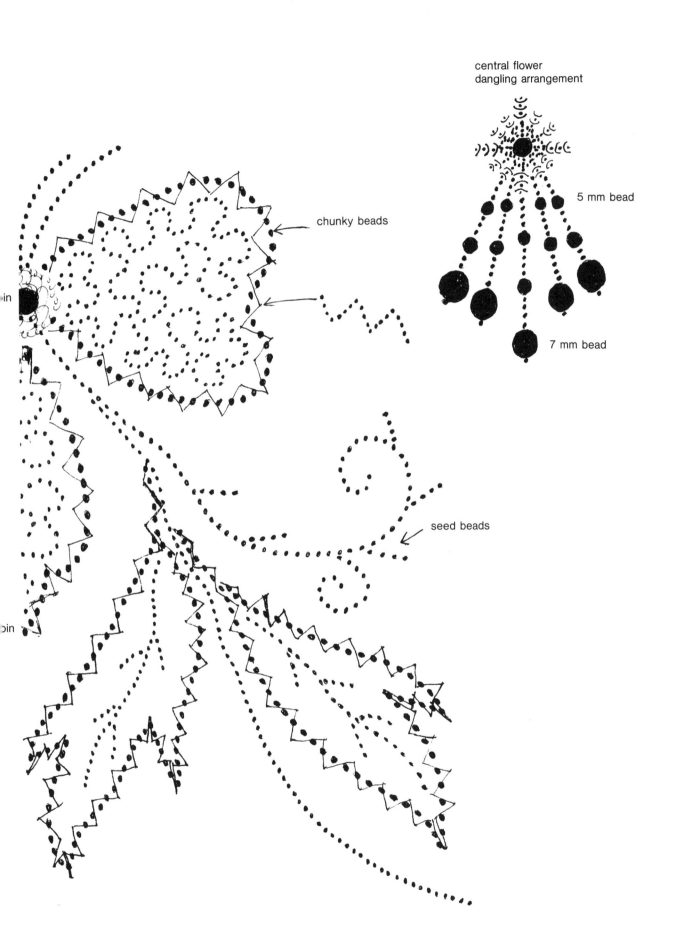

central flower
dangling arrangement

5 mm bead

7 mm bead

chunky beads

seed beads

5. *Peter Pan collar*

You will need

36 cm (14'') ring frame
Iridescent seed beads
Gold seed beads
Iridescent size 2 bugle beads
Cream pearls
0.5 m (½ yd) silk (colour of choice)
Matching thread

Method

1. Position the fabric wrong side up in the ring frame, centring the grains and stretching the fabric evenly and very taught. Tighten the screw.
2. Position the ring frame on the edge of the table, placing the covered brick weight over the edge of the frame.
3. Place the free-running thread on the holder.
4. Outline the shape of the collar pieces with a tacking thread.
5. Thread the iridescent seed beads onto the free-running thread and discard the bead-thread.
6. Holding the thread in your left hand underneath the frame and the tambour needle in the right hand, insert the needle and bring up the thread at the outer edge of the first collar piece. Make 2 tiny chain stitches (thread only) to anchor.
7. Move the iridescent beads up to the fabric, holding them between the thumb and forefinger. Holding the tambour needle upright with the screw facing to the right, insert the needle and make another chain stitch, catching the thread between the beads. Bring this up through the fabric, turning the needle as you do so to make a chain stitch the size of the seed bead.
8. Continue working the chain stitch with seed beads around the outside edge of the collar and finish with 2 tiny stitches to anchor.
9. Work another row inside the first row using gold seed beads.
10. Thread the iridescent size 2 bugle beads and work these in a zigzag, making a support stitch between each bead. Work 4 gold seed beads into each V of size 2 bugle beads as in sketch, with 4 beads together inside each V, again using the support stitch.

11. After completing the border, thread the iridescent seed beads and work a small Cornaly crazy design all over the collar.

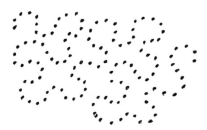

12. Work a second collar piece to match.
13. Remove the beading from the frame and cut around the outside edge leaving a 1 cm (⅜'') turning. Turn the fabric back to the first row of beads. With a single thread in a sewing needle tack the turning in place. Cut a piece of silk lining the same size as the beaded collar. Turn in the outer edge of the lining to match the outer edge of the collar. Slip stitch together all around the edge.
14. Sew a 4 mm cream pearl into each V by hand after all the beading on the frame is completed.
15. To finish the collars, cut a length of fabric on the bias 1 cm (⅜'') wide and sew this close to the beading on the neck edge. Turn back and hand sew neatly.
16. Return to the outside edge and using double thread, string together 9 gold seed beads and sew onto the collar, making a looped edge to give a picot look.

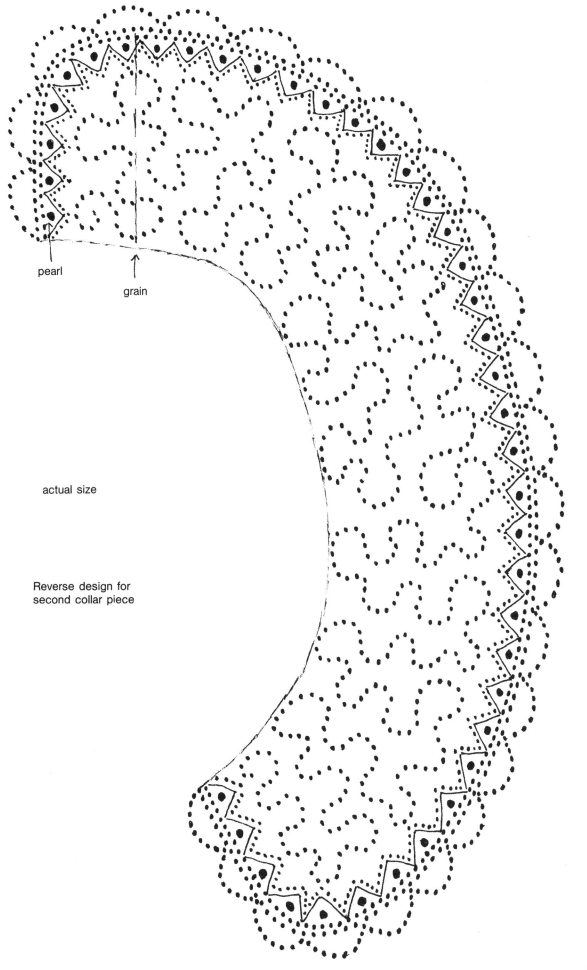

pearl

grain

actual size

Reverse design for
second collar piece

6. Working with wool and metallic threads

You will need

36 cm (14'') ring frame
A few metres of fine white wool (2-ply or equivalent)
Red seed beads
Silver metallic thread
1 red 7 mm cut bead
Red thread
Double-knit jersey
Thick (size 4) Cornaly needle
Fine (size 2) Cornaly needle
Fine interfacing

Method

1. Assemble the fabric on the ring frame, *right side up*. As this is jersey do not stretch it too tight, as it could bounce back and pucker when released. It would be advisable to use a very fine interfacing for this motif.

   Trace the flower and swirls on the right side facing you.

2. Working with the wool and metallic thread, which is done first, you will have the right side of the fabric facing you. To add the beads, just turn the ring frame over and work on the wrong side as usual. The wool and metallic threads are worked in chain stitch using the thick Cornaly needle.

The flower

3. Outline the flower motif with white wool. Hold the wool underneath the frame and insert the needle. Pull through to the right side, making a holding chain stitch.

   Continue with chain stitch all around the edge, keeping the stitches an even length.

4. Inside this edge, work another row of chain stitches using the silver metallic thread combined with red thread. This gives a variegated effect.

The scrolls

5. Work 3 rows of chain stitch in silver metallic thread, leaving enough space between the two close rows to fit a row of seed beads.

6. When you have completed all the thread work on the right side, turn the frame over to work the 3

rows of beads on the wrong side. Thread the red seed beads on the free-running thread on the left side and change from the thick Cornaly needle to a fine one.

7. Hold the thread underneath the frame and insert the needle. Pull through and hold. Make 2 tiny chain stitches (thread only) to anchor.

8. Move the beads to the fabric with the holder and needle facing to the right. Make a chain stitch, picking up a single bead and turning the needle as you make the chain stitch to hold the bead. Bead the 3 rows.

9. Return to the flower motif and fill it in with an all-over Cornaly design, leaving a space in the centre for a small flower.

beads

The centre flower

10. Turn the frame back to the right side. Sew the red cut bead in the centre of the flower using double thread and sewing twice. Using 9 beads for each loop, sew 4 loops evenly around the large bead. Make 4 more 9-bead loops overlapping the first 4 loops halfway.

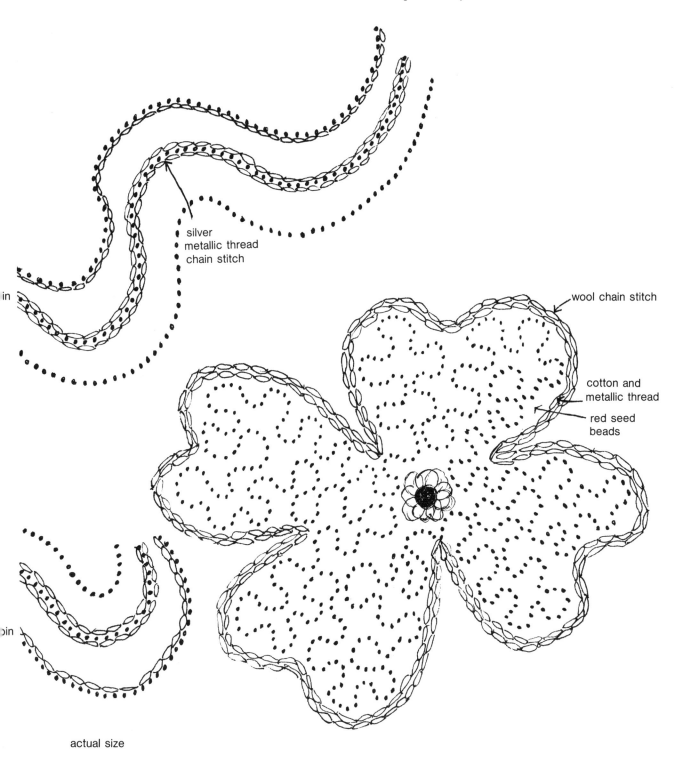

silver
metallic thread
chain stitch

wool chain stitch

cotton and
metallic thread

red seed
beads

in

ɔin

actual size

7. Victorian evening bag on silver silk

This is a tailored 'go-anywhere' bag.

You will need

36 cm (14'') ring frame
Silver bag frame 14 cm × 4.5 cm (5½'' × 1¾'')
30 cm (12'') silver coloured pure silk
30 cm (12'') white silk for the lining
0.5 m (½ yd) fine iron-on Vilene
Gunmetal 3-cut seed beads
Iridescent 3-cut crystal seed beads
Iridescent size 1 crystal bugle beads
Grey thread
Dressmaker's carbon paper

This pattern has been reduced to fit in the book. You will need to enlarge it by photocopying at 130% or by the grid method at 2 cm = 2.6 cm (1'' = 1⁵⁄₁₆'').

Note: This design can also be worked on the rectangular frame.

Method

1. Iron the Vilene to the wrong side of the fabric. Mark the shape of the bag, back and front the same, with a tacking thread and position the fabric, wrong side up, in the ring frame. (See page 47 for using a rectangular frame.)
2. Place the frame over a firm raised board or book, and lay a sheet of carbon paper and the traced design on the wrong side of the fabric. Press firmly with a pencil until you have marked all the lines.
3. Thread the gunmetal seed beads onto the free-running thread on the spool-holder. (As you will be using crystal, bugle and gunmetal beads, threading each of these onto separate spools will save a lot of time and trouble.)
4. Hold the thread from the gunmetal seed beads in the left hand underneath the frame, moving up to the fabric. With the tambour holder and needle in the right hand, insert the needle and pull the thread through the fabric and hold.
   Holding the needle upright and the screw facing to the right, make 2 tiny chain stitches and pull firm to anchor.
5. With the gunmetal seed beads work 2 rows of single beads all around the outside line of the bag.
6. Starting at the centre point of the rosette of radiating lines, bead a single row of gunmetal beads down the centre of the design. Work to the end, making a slight curve at the lower edge of the line of beads.
7. Work 2 lines of crystal seed beads, one on each side of the central gunmetal line, curving away at the bottom as in the design, then a row of gunmetal seed beads each side, following each on side with crystal bugle beads, then gunmetal seed beads and crystal seed beads. Continue alternating rows until the lower section is completed.

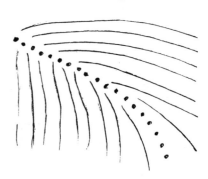

8. Bead one single row of gunmetal seed beads to divide the shape on the diagonals (see sketch). Alternate the 3 rows of beads as before, working diagonally across following the design. Work both sides to correspond.
9. Remove bag from the tambour frame and cut around, leaving a seam allowance of 1.5 cm (⅝'').
10. Cut the silk lining the same size as the bag and stitch side seams by machine. Pin the 2 pieces of beading together and with double thread sew together with back stitch, sewing close to the beads. Turn the bag to the right side and slip the lining in.
11. The top section of the bag is stitched to the bag frame. Pin the lining to the beading, turning seams inside, and slip-stitch around neatly. At each side of the bag (where the diagram indicates DO NOT BEAD) snip into the corners and slip-stitch lining to the bag. Ensure that all seams lie flat.

To sew the bag onto the frame
12. Thread a needle with 4 strands of thread for extra strength. Holding the bag to the frame, sew 3 times into the first hole of the frame, then twice into the following holes until the last hole is reached. Sew 3 times in the last hole and end off securely.
13. Thread together 3 gunmetal beads with double thread and sew from the bag to the holes on the frames. This will cover the thread and gives a finish to the bag.
14. Turn the bag inside out. Make a small pleat in the unbeaded corners below the hinges and stitch securely. This will make the bag pouch.

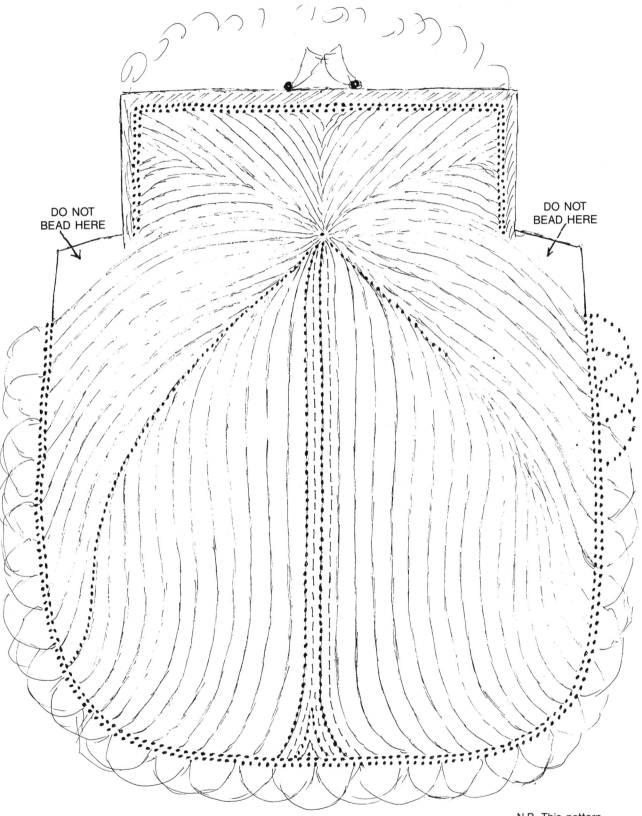

DO NOT
BEAD HERE

DO NOT
BEAD HERE

N.B. This pattern
must be enlarged

15. Using a double thread, sew 14 beads together in loops 10 mm (⅜'') apart around the outside edge of the bag. Work a second row, alternating the loops as in the sketch.

8. *Victorian evening bag on black silk*

You will need

36 cm (14'') ring frame
16 cm × 6 cm (6¼'' × 2½'') rectangular silver bag frame
32 cm (12½'') black satin and black silk for lining
32 cm (12½'') iron-on fine Vilene
Black 3-cut seed beads
White crystal 3-cut seed beads
Silver metal 3-cut seed beads
Iridescent chunky crystal beads
4 mm black cut beads
Black thread
Dressmaker's carbon paper

Note: This design can also be worked on the rectangular frame.

Method

1. Iron the Vilene to the wrong side of the black satin.
2. Trace the shape of the bag onto the Vilene, using a marking pencil, then trace around with a tacking thread. *Do not cut out*, but leave all in one piece for attaching to the frame.

   With the wrong side of the fabric facing upwards, assemble the fabric into the ring frame, keeping grains even and stretching fabric taut. (See page 47 for instructions for fixing fabric into a rectangular frame.)
3. Place a firm board or book underneath the fabric in the frame, lay the carbon paper over the fabric with the beading design and trace firmly with a pencil.
4. Thread about 1 metre (40'') of black seed beads onto the free-running thread on the spool-holder. Insert the tambour needle with holder on the outside line of the bag. Hold thread and make 2 tiny chain stitches to anchor (thread only). Move 1 bead singly to the fabric and make a chain stitch with 1 bead. Continue around the traced line. To end off make 2 tiny chain stitches to anchor (thread only).
5. Remember you are working from the wrong side, i.e. all the beads are underneath.
6. Thread silver seed beads to be worked inside the row of black beads. Insert the needle and make 2 chain stitches (thread only). Move 3 beads together, placing them flat against the fabric in a zigzag fashion and making 1 support stitch (thread only) at each point. Continue all around.

7. Bead all the scrolls using silver cut beads. Outline each scroll with single beads, then carefully fill each scroll, beading a close crazy stitch to cover the fabric. End each section by making 2 small anchor stitches (thread only).

8. Return to the centre section and outline each side with the iridescent chunky crystal beads, beading singly. Bead the single scroll lines with silver beads. Use white crystal beads to fill in all over and around the scrolls. See sketch on page 41.
9. Complete the beading by filling in all around the scrolls with black seed beads in a close crazy pattern.
10. It is optional whether you bead the design on both sides of the bag. If you prefer the second side can just be closely beaded all over with black beads.

Sewing the bag together

11. Remove from the frame. Cut all around leaving 12 mm (¾'') seam allowance. Pin together, keeping the bead edges close together. Hand sew with a back stitch using a double thread.
12. Cut lining the same size and stitch the seams around by machine. Slide the lining into the bag.
13. To sew the top section onto the bag frame, turn the satin around the edge of the black beads and tack around it. Turn the seam allowance of the lining and slip-stitch together.
14. The bag is now ready to sew onto the frame. Use 4 strands of thread together as the junction with the metal frame needs to be very strong. Hold the bag to the frame, starting from the lower hole on the side of the frame.
15. With needle and thread, sew from the bag to the frame, 3 times into the one hole. Then move to the next hole, sewing twice. Continue sewing from bag to frame twice into each hole, keeping very even until you have come to the last hole. Sew into this hole 3 times and end off securely.
16. Return to the first hole on the frame and using a double thread, sew 5 black seed beads together

Rose motif worked in several pinks on a black background (page 20)

Spider flower motif worked in icy blues on blue georgette in a ring frame (page 22)

Wild rose design (page 24)
worked on the rectangular tambour
frame

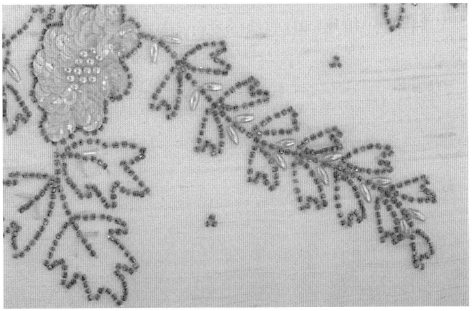

Detail

Bow motif worked in dramatic red and black in a ring frame (page 27)

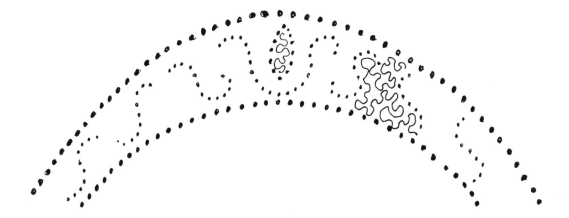

from the bag to the frame in a looped fashion to cover all thread work.

17. Turn the bag inside out. On each side where the pattern says DO NOT BEAD, make a pleat and sew securely with a double thread. Turn the bag back to the right side and the pleats will pouch the bag.

18. To finish the bag, add a looped fringe all around the outside edge. With a double thread, insert the needle 5 cm below the frame. Thread together 22 black seed beads, one 5 mm cut black bead and 13 silver beads; insert the needle back through the black cut bead. Thread a further 22 black beads and take back to the bag. Make a support stitch between each loop of beads. You now have a very glamorous Victorian· bag!

*Victorian evening bag on black silk
(instructions page 36)*

actual size

black 3-cut →
seed beads

chunky iridescent crystal beads

silver metallic
3-cut seed beads

DO NOT
BEAD HERE

DO NOT
BEAD HERE

42

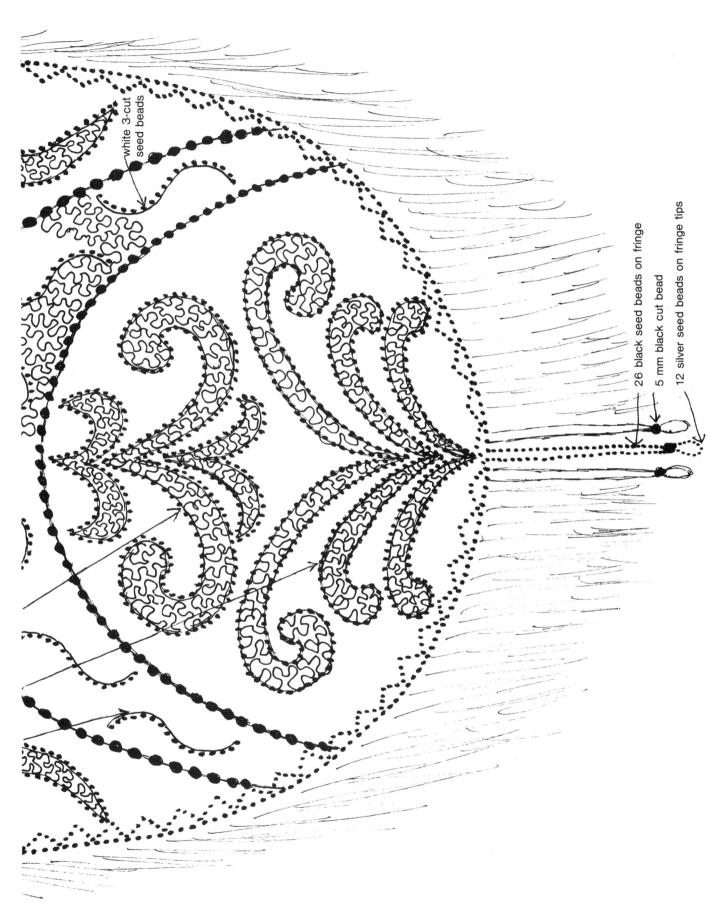

white 3-cut seed beads

26 black seed beads on fringe

5 mm black cut bead

12 silver seed beads on fringe tips

43

9. Small Victorian dolly bag

You will need
36 cm (14'') ring frame
0.25 m (¼ yd) dark grey silk
0.25 m (¼ yd) white silk lining
1 small dome-shaped frame, 13 cm × 7 cm
    (5'' × 2¾'') or a rectangular frame 12 cm × 5 cm
    (4¾'' × 2'')
Gunmetal 3-cut beads
Matching thread
Iron-on fine Vilene

This small Victorian bag would look very smart beaded all over in jet, bronze or gold (depending on the colour of the frame). Use matching background fabric for the beads.

Note: This design can also be worked on the rectangular frame.

Method
1. Iron the Vilene onto the wrong side of the silk. Trace the shape of the bag all around with tacking thread. *Do not cut out.*
2. With the wrong side of the fabric facing upwards, assemble the fabric into the ring frame, keeping grains even and stretching fabric taut. (See page 47 for instructions for fixing fabric into a rectangular frame.)
3. There is no set design for this bag as it is nearly all worked freehand in a continuous spiral of seed beads worked singly.
4. The small section of beads above the circle inside the frame area is beaded first. Insert the tambour holder with needle, beading one row of beads all around the edge with single beads. Remember to anchor the two tiny stitches (thread only) when starting and finishing each section of beads.
5. Bead all around the outline of the bag with single beads. Bead a complete circle, 1 row of single beads, using the ends of the frame as a guide for the size of the circle. This leaves a space underneath the frame to be filled in with lines from one end of the frame to the other.
7. Starting from the central point of the circle, work around an ever-increasing spiral of single beads, keeping the lines very even.
8. The bag is finished with a double loop fringe all around the edge. This is worked on both sides and can be done while the bag is still on the frame.
9. Use two spools of thread, one on each of two spool holders, to give a double thread for the fringing. Mark an 8 cm (3'') line on your work surface (make a mark on the webbing if you are using the rectangular frame) and thread about 1 metre (40'') of gunmetal beads on the double threads. With the tambour holder and needle, make 2 tiny stitches to anchor. Measure 8 cm (3'') of beads and loop these to the fabric, making a chain stitch and a small support stitch beside it. Continue all around the bag, beading close to the outside row of beads.
10. Bead the other side of the bag to match. Remove from the frame and cut out, leaving a seam allowance of 12 mm (½''). Cut out the lining the same shape and size as the bag. Machine stitch the lining and slip it into the bag. Pin the bag together and using a doubled matching coloured thread, sew up the bag using a back stitch close to the edge of the beads, and keeping the fringing hanging neatly. Turn in the edges of the lining and bag together on the top section and slip stitch around neatly.

Using 4 strands of thread, sew the bag to the frame, making sure it fits very evenly. At the side sections where the pattern says DO NOT BEAD, gather across with small running stitches to pouch the bag.

To make the bag with a rectangular frame, use the same instructions but follow the sketch on page 46.

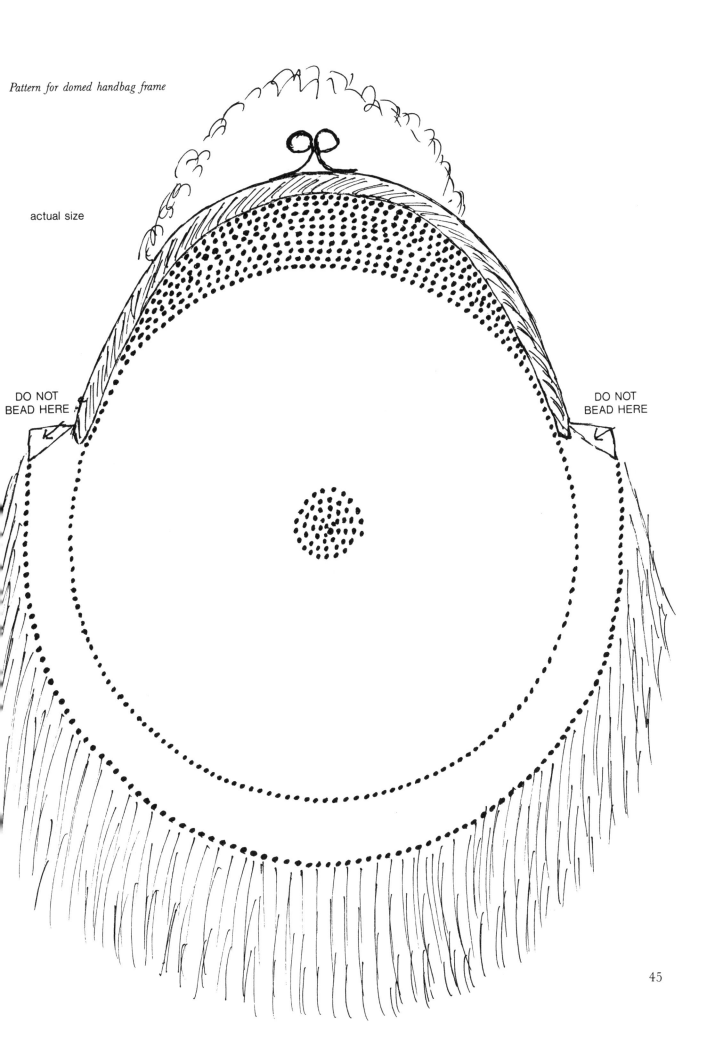

Pattern for domed handbag frame

actual size

DO NOT
BEAD HERE

DO NOT
BEAD HERE

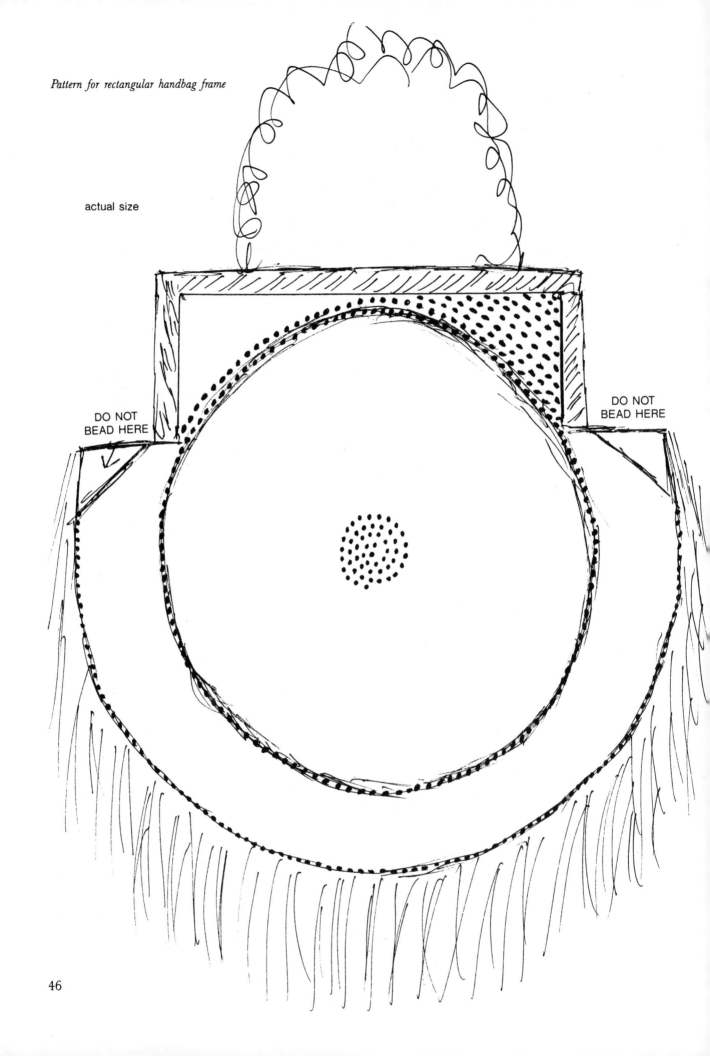

Pattern for rectangular handbag frame

actual size

DO NOT
BEAD HERE

DO NOT
BEAD HERE

THE RECTANGULAR TAMBOUR FRAME

Larger tambour-beaded items such as blouses and frocks, particularly those with all over designs, must be worked on a large rectangular frame. This kind of frame is not available commercially, but can easily be made by a handyperson.

As the fabric to be worked on must be kept very taut, and you need to work with both hands, the frame must be free-standing. It is made from dressed oregon or a similar timber.

You will need

2 lengths oregon 1370 mm × 50 mm × 50 mm (54'' × 2'' × 2'')
2 lengths oregon 710 mm × 30 mm × 20 mm (28'' × 1⅛'' × ⅞'')
4 × 150 mm (6'') nails
1.1 m (43'') × 40 mm (1½'') webbing
2 rolls 25 mm (1'') tape
16 mm (⅝'') flat-head tacks

Cut four rectangular slot holes through each end of the two 1370 mm (54'') lengths approximately 100–150 mm (4''–6'') from the ends, to allow the two 710 mm (28'') lengths to be passed through. The nails fit through both slot holes.

1. The shorter lengths must be drilled with multiple matching holes large enough for a 150 mm (6'') nail to pass through easily. See sketch.
2. The corners of the long pieces must be slightly rounded with a small plane or spoke shave (and sanded smooth) to protect the fabric when it's stretched taut on the frame.
3. Fix a length of webbing to each of the longer lengths of wood, on the outer edges, with the flat-headed tacks, hammering the tacks well into the wood so that fabric will not snag on them. The frame is now ready for use.

Setting up the frame

1. Before you attach the fabric to the frame, mark the shape of the garment pattern on the fabric and trace all around with a tacking thread. *Do not cut out the garment.*
2. Tack the pattern piece onto the webbing on each long length of wood with strong thread, having the wrong side of the fabric facing you. On some designs you will have a lot of fabric to handle. You can roll part of it to one side of the wood with sheets of tissue paper to protect the fabric. Roll the amount of material to make working comfortable.
3. Pass the short woods through the rectangular slots of the long woods, using the 4 nails to anchor them in position. Loop the tapes around the short woods and pin to the fabric in several places. Stretch the fabric horizontally, ensuring the grains run even in both directions. You may have to adjust the tapes until you get this right. The fabric *must* be taut.
4. If fabric becomes a little slack while you are embroidering, simply move the long woods a little further apart, moving the nails into the next holes. This will keep the fabric taut.
5. Having marked the design you will be using onto tracing paper, place some dressmaker's carbon paper onto the fabric, then pin the design on top of this ready to transfer.
6. Rest the frame on a firm board so you can press

strongly with a pencil to transfer the design onto the fabric.

7. As you will be using both hands for beading, support the frame between two stands, trestles or stools at a comfortable height to work on.

8. Before you start, place the spool of free-running thread on one of the nails on the left-hand side and thread the beads onto it. (This frame has in-built spool holders!)

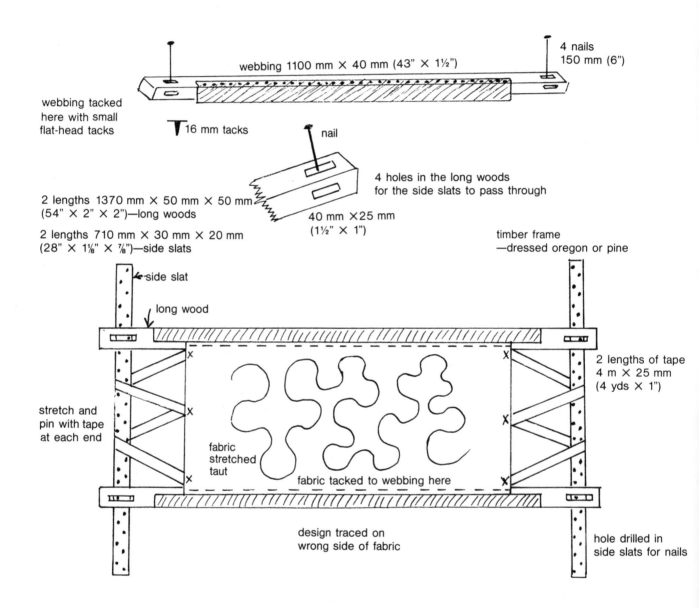

webbing 1100 mm × 40 mm (43" × 1½")

4 nails 150 mm (6")

webbing tacked here with small flat-head tacks

16 mm tacks

nail

4 holes in the long woods for the side slats to pass through

2 lengths 1370 mm × 50 mm × 50 mm (54" × 2" × 2")—long woods

2 lengths 710 mm × 30 mm × 20 mm (28" × 1⅛" × ⅞")—side slats

40 mm × 25 mm (1½" × 1")

timber frame —dressed oregon or pine

side slat

long wood

2 lengths of tape 4 m × 25 mm (4 yds × 1")

stretch and pin with tape at each end

fabric stretched taut

fabric tacked to webbing here

design traced on wrong side of fabric

hole drilled in side slats for nails

The rectangular tambour frame set up for working

48

Both pieces of the Peter Pan collar can be worked in the ring frame (page 30)

49

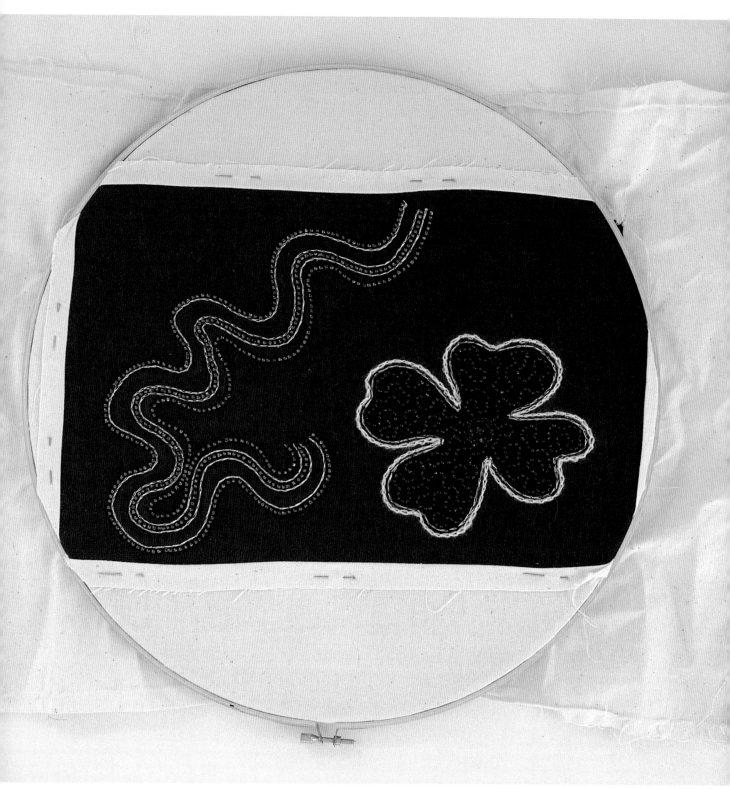

This bold design using wool, metallic threads and beads (page 32) is worked on double-knit jersey using a calico support

Opposite: Victorian evening bag is worked in gunmetal and crystal beads on silver silk (page 34)

RECTANGULAR FRAME PROJECTS

10. Ice-blue chiffon overblouse

You will need

Rectangular frame
Aqua 3-cut seed beads
Pale blue iridescent cup sequins
4 mm iridescent cut crystal beads
Pale blue 3 mm seed pearls
Pale blue pure silk chiffon
Pale blue silk or satin lining
Matching thread
Dressmaker's carbon paper

This hip-length overblouse has a 4.5 cm (1¾'') beaded border around the neck, sleeve edges and hemline to set off the allover lattice-work design. The lattice is interrupted with a tiny paisley design, worked with tiny sequinned scrolls down the centre.

Chiffon is a very delicate fabric to bead. A soft silk lining backing the chiffon helps to hold the beading in place. Each seam must be sewn by hand with a fine back stitch.

A matching Thai silk skirt would make a very elegant outfit.

Note This pattern has had to be reduced to fit in the book, so you will need to enlarge it again by photocopying at 160% or by the grid method at 2 cm = 3.2 cm (1'' = 1⅝'').

Opposite: This elaborate Victorian evening bag is worked in silver, black and crystal beads on black silk (page 36)

Method

1. Choose a simple dropped shoulder pattern with a round neck. Lay the front and back pattern pieces on the chiffon and trace around the shapes with a tacking thread. *Do not cut out*, but leave the fabric all in one piece for attaching to the tambour frame. Tack the ends of the fabric to the webbing on the long woods, with the wrong side facing you. Use a strong thread for this as the fabric must be stretched taut.

   The grain of the fabric should run vertically, from long wood to long wood.

   Roll up the excess chiffon beside one of the long woods using sheets of tissue paper to protect the fabric. Leave a comfortable amount of fabric to work on.

2. Pass the side woods through the slots and stretch the chiffon tight, inserting the nails to fix the long woods in position. Loop the tapes around the side woods, pin and stretch in position on the edges of the fabric (see diagram). The vertical and horizontal grains of the fabric must be stretched evenly in each direction.

3. Work the neck and armhole borders, starting from the neck edge. Thread the blue seed beads onto a spool of matching free-running machine thread positioned on one of the left nails. Work with approximately 1 metre (40'') of threaded beads at a time.

4. Holding the thread with the left hand and the tambour holder and needle in the right hand, pull thread through to the wrong side. Hold and make two tiny chain stitches to anchor (thread only). Moving a seed bead to the material, make a chain stitch the size of the tiny seed bead. Continue all

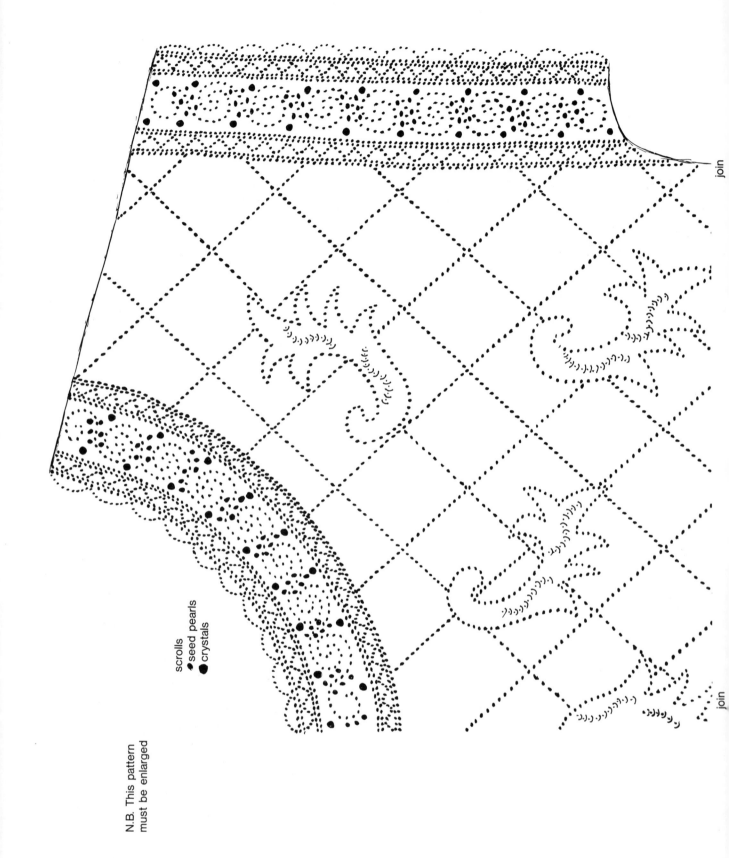

scrolls
seed pearls
crystals

join

join

N.B. This pattern
must be enlarged

around the neckline, then bead a second line, keeping this close and even to the first row of beads.

5. With a tracing pencil mark a line 1 cm (⅜'') in from the neck edge. Moving 3 beads together in flat formation, working a zigzag between the line and the beaded work. Make a tiny support stitch (thread only) at each point of the zigzag. Bead another two lines below the zigzag.

6. With the tracing pencil mark another line 4.5 cm (1¾'') in from the neck edge and work a further 2 rows of seed beads. Repeat the zigzag and the 2 rows of beads.

7. Work the same border around the sleeve edges and the hemline. In the open spaces between these beaded borders work small scrolls of seed beads with 3 seed pearls and single crystals added to highlight the beads.

8. When the borders are completed trace the lattice and paisley design onto the main body of the blouse. Pin a sheet of carbon paper and the traced design to the fabric. Place the frame over a firm board to make it easier to press the pencil down.

9. All the single lines of lattice and paisley are beaded with seed beads, working with a single bead at a time, making 1 chain stitch for each. Work 2 tiny scrolls of pale blue sequins in the centre of each paisley.

10. Once the front of the blouse is completed, remove the tapes and nails and slide out the side woods. Roll up the beaded work with tissue paper to protect the beading. Then unroll the fabric for the back, using the same procedure as before to assemble the frame. Repeat the beading on the back of the blouse and remove from the frame.

To sew the blouse together

11. Cut out all around the tacking line leaving a seam allowance of 1.5 cm (⅝''). Allow 5.5 cm (2'') for the hem. Lay the blouse pieces on the lining, pinning and tacking together before cutting out the lining. Allow the same large hem allowance for the lining. The tacking will hold without slipping.

12. Pin all seams together, matching all the borders. Turn up the bottom hemlines of chiffon and lining and sew separately, using a neat slip stitch. These hems are pinned and sewn into the side seams, matching all the borders.

Sew all seams by hand with a small back stitch.

13. Cut a length of lining fabric on the bias, 2 cm (¾'') wide, for the neck facing. Sew this by hand close to the first row of beads, then trim away and turn under using a neat small slip stitch.

14. Hem the seam allowance around the edge of the sleeve.

15. With beading face down, press all seams gently into a towel, using a warm iron.

16. Finally, add a looped edge around all the borders to finish the blouse.

Around the neck and sleeve edge, thread together 11 seed beads with double thread and sew 12 mm (½'') loops to create a scalloped effect.

17. The hemline has a double scalloped edge. The first line of scallops is a repeat of the neck and sleeve, i.e. 11 seed beads. The second line of scallops is worked behind the first line. Thread together 12 seed beads, a 4 mm crystal bead and 12 seed beads. Loop these coming from the centres of the first loops (see sketch).

11. 1920s paisley design on black chiffon

You will need

Jet 3-cut seed beads
Jade 3-cut seed beads
Iridescent oatmeal 3-cut seed beads
9 ct gold size 1 bugle beads
9 ct gold seed beads
Black pure silk chiffon
Black silk for lining
Matching thread
Dressmaker's carbon paper

Note This pattern has had to be reduced to fit in the book, so you will need to enlarge it again by photocopying at 175% or by the grid method at 2 cm = 3.5 cm (1'' = 1¾'').

Method

1. Adjust pattern to your measurements. Lay the pattern on the fabric and trace all around with a tacking thread. *Do not cut out.* This must now be attached to the rectangular tambour frame following the instructions on page 47.
2. The blouse is embroidered with an all-over variegated paisley design. Reverse the pattern on pages 58–59 to give you the full pattern for the other half. Trace the design onto the fabric from a large sheet of tracing paper the shape and size of the blouse.
3. Place the tracing paper on the wrong side of the chiffon with a sheet of white or yellow carbon paper between the design and the fabric. Rest the fabric stretched on the frame on a firm board as this will make it easier to trace the design onto the fabric. Press firmly with a pencil to transfer the design onto the blouse. About half the length of the blouse should be comfortable to bead at the same time.
4. Thread about 1 metre (40'') of jet 3-cut seed beads onto a spool of black thread attached to a nail on the left-hand side of the tambour frame.

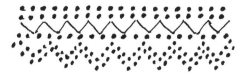

1st row: jet seed beads worked singly.
2nd row: iridescent oatmeal seed beads worked singly.

3rd row: size 1 gold bugle beads worked in a zigzag fashion (see sketch).
4th row: jade seed beads worked singly.
5th row: work 3 jet seed beads together in a zigzag fashion, taking a support stitch after every three beads.
6th row: repeat the zigzag working with gold seed beads.

Work the borders around the neck and armholes first.

Repeat the border at the hemline, with the jet beads on the lower edge.

6. The paisleys are varied, using different beads at ornate angles. Follow the instructions for each paisley, numbered 1 to 9 on the diagram.

Beads of 6 different colours are used to embroider this design. Have 6 spools of black thread with each of the individually coloured beads threaded—this will make the work easier.

Paisley 1:
Bead jet seed beads singly around the outline; inside the line bead jade beads singly. In the centre, bead 3 oatmeal beads together in a zigzag, remembering to make the support stitch with each 3 beads. Bead the small scrolls with single beads, the outside line with jet, the inside with oatmeal seed beads. Repeat this on each paisley marked **1**.

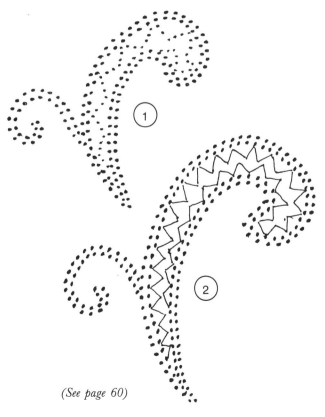

(See page 60)

join A

join B

Reverse pattern to complete

N.B. This pattern
must be enlarged

A

B

Paisley 2:

Bead jet seed beads singly around the outline, oatmeal seed beads singly inside. Work the centre using gold size 1 bugle beads in zigzag. Bead small scroll with jet beads singly on the outside, oatmeal seed beads on the inside. Repeat this on each paisley marked **2**.

Paisley 3 (two versions):

Bead jet seed beads singly on the outline, oatmeal seed beads singly on the inside line. Repeat this on each paisley marked **3**.

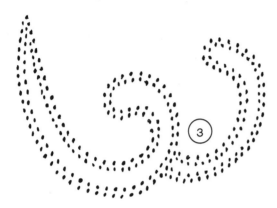

Paisley 4:

Bead jet seed beads singly around outline. On the inside line, bead oatmeal beads singly. Centre, bead 3 gold beads together in a zigzag. This paisley has 2 scrolls, one large and one small. Bead the large scroll outlined in jet seed beads, inside with jade seed beads, the small scroll outlined in jet seed beads, inside with gold seed beads. Repeat this on each paisley marked **4**.

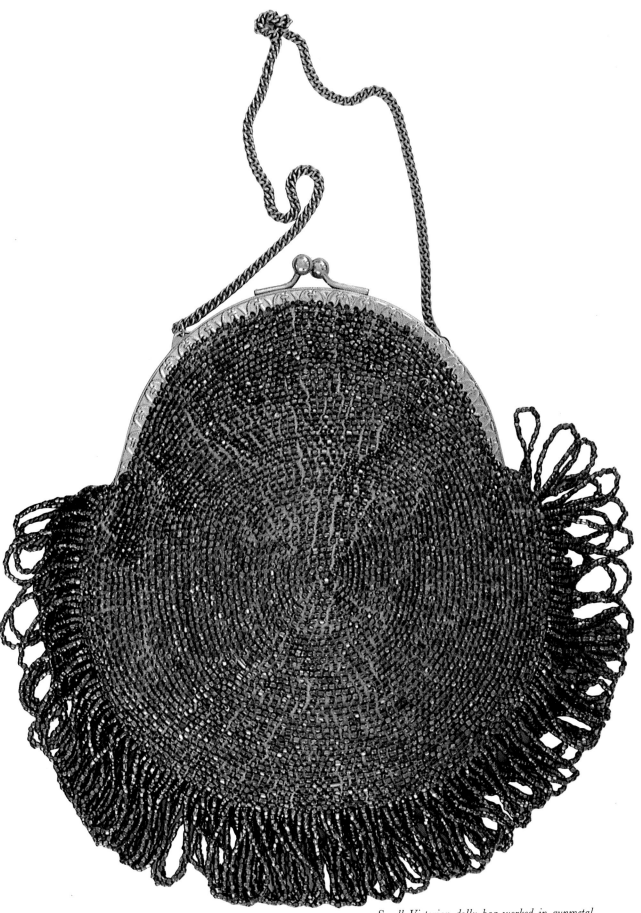

Small Victorian dolly bag worked in gunmetal
3-cut beads on dark grey silk (page 44)

Ice-blue chiffon overblouse (page 53)

*Elaborate 1920s paisley design on
black chiffon (page 57)*

Pink silk overblouse with unusual 'lightning strikes' interspersed with paisley patterns (page 67)

Paisley 5:
This paisley has two versions. Bead jet seed beads singly around outline. Inside line, bead oatmeal beads singly. Centre, bead 3 gold beads together in a zigzag fashion.

Bead the large scroll with jet seed beads on the outside, jade seed beads on the inside. Bead the small scroll with jet seed beads on the outside, on the inside gold seed beads. Repeat for each paisley marked **5**.

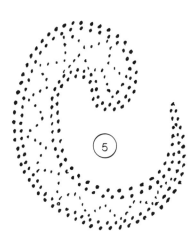

Paisley 6:
Bead jet seed beads singly around outline. Inside line, bead oatmeal beads singly. Centre, bead 3 oatmeal beads together in a zigzag fashion. Repeat for each paisley marked **6**.

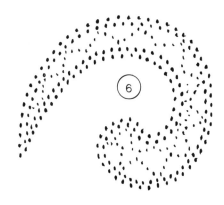

Paisley 7:
Outline with jet seed beads, inside bead with gold size 1 bugle beads in a zigzag fashion. Repeat for each paisley marked **7**.

Paisley 8:
Bead the outline with jet seed beads, the inside with jade seed beads.

Paisley 9:

The 3-petalled flowers are outlined using jade seed beads. The petals are filled in with gold seed beads worked with the close 'crazy' Cornaly stitch. The small scroll is omitted on some of the flowers.

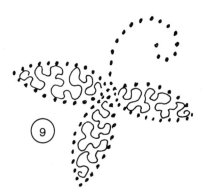

The fringing:

7. Thread about 1 metre (40'') of jet seed beads onto double thread coming from each of 2 spools of black thread positioned on the left-hand nails. Make a 13 cm (5'') measurement mark on the webbing. The loops of fringing come from the row of jet beads at the hem. Insert the needle, making 2 tiny chain stitches (thread only). Measure 13 cm (5'') of beads and loop these to the fabric. Make 1 chain stitch then a tiny chain stitch (thread only) to anchor each loop of fringing.

8. Using double thread and a tiny anchoring stitch will make the fringe strong, essential because there is a lot of wear on this part of a garment.

9. To complete the garment, remove from the frame and cut out, leaving a 12 mm (½'') seam allowance all around the beading. Lay the chiffon carefully onto the piece of silk lining and tack together. Leave a border width for the chiffon hem and 2.5 cm (1'') for the lining hem. These hems are turned up separately.

   Pin then sew shoulders and sideseams together by hand, using a small back stitch. Match all the borders. Turn hemlines and slip stitch neatly.

   Measure the neck and armholes and cut a length of silk on the bias, 15 mm (⅝'') wide.

   Hand sew this around close to the beaded border with a back stitch, then turn to the inside and slip stitch the facing.

10. To complete the garment, use a double thread and thread together 9 jet seed beads. Sew these in a looped fashion around the neck and armholes for a picot-edged effect.

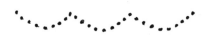

12. *Pink silk overblouse*

You will need
Pink silk
Pink 3-cut seed beads
Pink crystal cup sequins
Pink 3 mm seed pearls
Matching thread
Dressmaker's carbon paper

Note This pattern has had to be reduced to fit in the book, so you will need to enlarge it again by photocopying at 160% or by the grid method at 2 cm = 3.2 cm (1'' = 1⅝'').

I have used a combination of 'lightning strikes' and paisleys in the design on this lovely silk overblouse, adding fringing around the sleeve edges and the hemline. A matching skirt would make it into an elegant gown.

Method
1. Choose a simple dropped shoulder pattern with a round neckline to suit your measurements.

   Lay the front and back pattern pieces on the fabric and trace around them with a tacking thread. *Do not cut out*, but leave the fabric in one piece for attaching to the tambour frame. Assemble the fabric in the frame following the directions on page 47, centring the grains and pulling the fabric taut.

   Roll up the half of the fabric you are not working on one side, using tissue paper to protect the fabric. Leave a comfortable amount of fabric to work on.
2. Work the neck and armhole borders first, starting from the neck edge. Thread the pink seed beads onto a spool of matching free-running machine thread placed on one of the left-hand nails. Work with approximately 1 metre (40'') of beads at a time. Make 2 tiny chain stitches to anchor (thread only), then bead one row of beads around the neckline.

   At the end of each section, make 2 small anchor stitches (thread only). From this row of beads, move 3 beads together in flat formation, working a zigzag. Make a tiny support stitch (thread only) after each group of 3 beads is worked to hold the beads firm.

3. Repeat this edge around the sleeve edges and the edge of the hemline.

4. To work the fringes, which are done next, use 2 spools of thread, one on each left hand nail, to give you a double thread. Thread at least a metre (40'') of beads onto the double thread.
5. Make an 8 cm (3'') measurement mark on the webbing to measure each length of fringing as you bead.
6. Pull the threads through the fabric and make 2 chain stitches (thread only) to anchor. Measure 8 cm (3'') of beads, making the first loop of the fringe with a chain stitch, then the next loop with a chain stitch, then a further support stitch with thread only. Take another 8 cm (3'') of beads and continue along the sleeve edges and the hemline.

   This fringing takes a lot of beads; you will have to rethread about every 7 cm (2¾'').
7. When the borders and the fringing are completed, trace the design onto the main body of the blouse, using dressmaker's carbon paper pinned to the fabric under the traced design. Place the frame over a firm board underneath and press firmly with a pencil.
8. Bead around the edges of all the paisley designs with the seed beads, moving 3 beads to the line and working a raised up zigzag. This is achieved by using a small chain stitch together with a small support stitch which keeps the beads raised off the fabric.
9. Bead the 'lightning strike' lines, moving one bead at a time with 1 chain stitch.
10. Return to the paisley designs and fill in all the centres, outlining with single beads and an inner row of crystal sequins, and filling the remainder of the centre with a few seed pearls.

11. The spotting is added later, when the garment is finished.

join A

pattern continues on page 70

N.B. This pattern
must be enlarged

join

join

join

pattern continues on page 71

join B

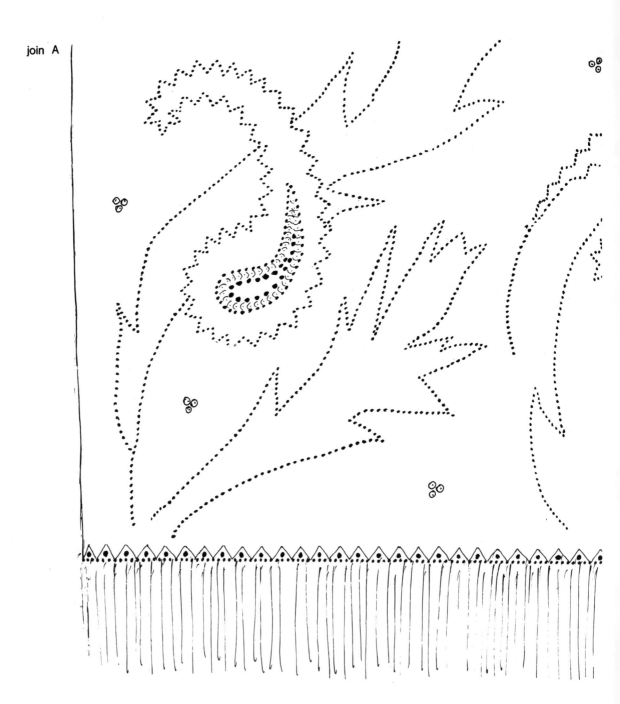

12. Once the front of the blouse is completed, remove the tapes and nails, slide out the side woods and roll away the front beading with more tissue paper to protect it. Then unroll the fabric for the back and assemble it into the frame. Repeat the beading design.

To sew the blouse together
13. Cut out all around the tacking line leaving a seam allowance of 1.5 cm (⅝'') and allowing 5.5 cm (2'') for the lower hemline.

14. Cut a facing for the neck and tack around the neck very close to the beads. You will be able to sew this seam by machine, using a zipper foot to get close to the beads. Stitch with care. Tack all seams

before stitching, matching all border edges. Turn back neck facing and catch with slip stitches.
15. Stitch lower hemline with a neat slip stitch. Finally,

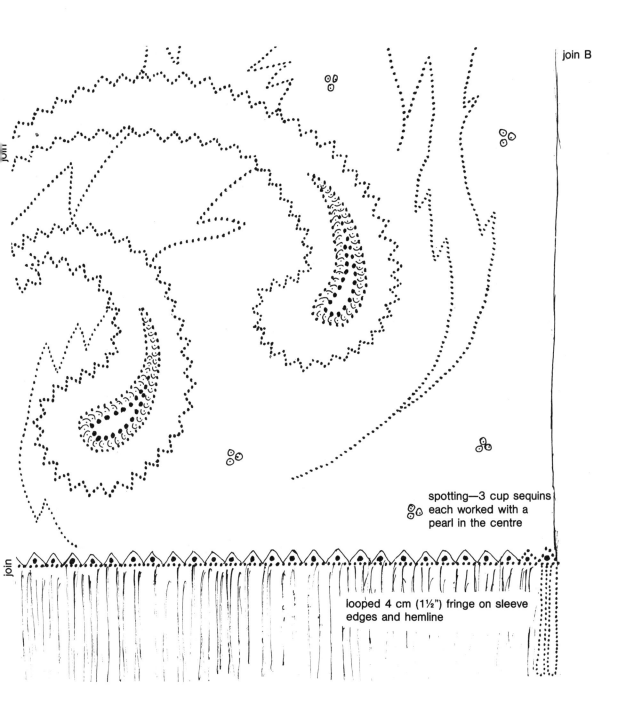

spotting—3 cup sequins
each worked with a
pearl in the centre

looped 4 cm (1½") fringe on sleeve
edges and hemline

join

finish the edges of the borders by sewing a seed
pearl into each V of the zigzag.

16. Sew spotting where marked on the design: sew 1
sequin, picking up from the wrong side, then 1
pearl, and insert the needle back through the sequin
to anchor. Sew in clusters of 3.

Suppliers

Tambour needles and beads can be purchased from:

AUSTRALIA

(042) 341 4775*
Mail order—needles sent

Photios Bros Pty Ltd*
66 Druitt Street
Sydney NSW 2000
(02) 267 1428

Creative Bead Imports*
255 South Terrace
South Fremantle WA 6162
(09) 336 1525 Fax (09) 335 3957

GREAT BRITAIN

Creative Beadcraft Ltd*
Denmark Works
Beaumond End
Amersham
Bucks HP7 0RX England
049 471 5606

London address:
20 Beak Street
London WIR 3HA
071 629 9964

Ring frames can be purchased at all craft shops.

All the beads, sequins, pearls and trimmings shown in this book can be purchased from:

AUSTRALIA

Photios Bros Pty Limited*
66 Druitt Street
Sydney NSW 2000
(02) 267 1428

Comprehensive ranges of beads and findings are also carried by:

Bead Co. of Australia*
497 Elizabeth Street
Surry Hills 2010
(02) 318 2775

Beads Galore Pty Ltd
25a Playfair Street
The Rocks, Sydney 2000
(02) 247 5946

Stadia Handcrafts
85 Elizabeth Street
Paddington 2021
(02) 328 7900

The Bead Co. of Victoria*
336 Smith Street
Collingwood 3066
(03) 419 0636

Maria George Pty Ltd
179 Flinders Lane
Melbourne 3000
(03) 650 1151   (03) 650 4117

Glamour 'N' Glitter Pty Ltd
49 Atkinson Street
Chadstone 3148
(03) 563 1300

Bead & Trimming Co.*
69 Elizabeth Street
Brisbane 4000
(07) 221 1315

The Bead Shop*
190 Goodwood Road
Millswood 5034
(08) 373 1296

NEW ZEALAND

The Stitching Company
29 Nugent Street
Auckland
(09) 366 6040

Beatrice Products
PO Box 15021
Christchurch
(03) 388 8119

USA

Bead Works*
105 N. Cortez Street
Prescott AZ 86301
602 771 0921

indicates mail order service available.

Many department stores and haberdashers also carry a range of beads.